Conditions of the

HEART

Some promises need to be broken!

Noel Sanabria

WESTBOW®
PRESS
A DIVISION OF THOMAS NELSON
& ZONDERVAN

Selection from The Heart Revolution used by permission of the Baker Publishing Group.

Credit for song lyrics: Ricardo Sanchez.

Scripture quotations taken from the Holy Bible, New Living Translation, Copyright © 1996, 2004. Used by permission of Tyndale House Publishers, Inc., Wheaton, Illinois 60189. All rights reserved.

Scripture quotations taken from the New American Standard Bible®, Copyright © 1960, 1962, 1963, 1968, 1971, 1972, 1973, 1975, 1977, 1995 by The Lockman Foundation. Used by permission. (www.Lockman.org)

Scripture taken from the Holy Bible, NEW INTERNATIONAL VERSION®. Copyright © 1973, 1978, 1984 by Biblica, Inc. All rights reserved worldwide. Used by permission. NEW INTERNATIONAL VERSION® and NIV® are registered trademarks of Biblica, Inc. Use of either trademark for the offering of goods or services requires the prior written consent of Biblica US, Inc.

WestBow Press books may be ordered through booksellers or by contacting:
WestBow Press
A Division of Thomas Nelson & Zondervan
1663 Liberty Drive
Bloomington, IN 47403
www.westbowpress.com
1 (866) 928-1240

ISBN: 978-1-4908-6928-5 (sc)
ISBN: 978-1-4908-6929-2 (e)

Library of Congress Control Number: 2015902116

Printed in the United States of America.

WestBow Press rev. date: 02/13/2015

Contents

Foreword

Millions of people struggle with conditions of the heart. In his book Pastor Noel helps you uncover your own state of mind by sharing candidly about his life.

By reading the pages of "Conditions of The Heart" you will understand that living with the absence of transparency has negative effects in your life. The author provides ways to steer your thoughts and feelings away from negativity and self-doubt, towards faith and hope.

Through the reflection questions at the end of each chapter and the memory verse, you will learn a practical technique and exercise for establishing new worry-free patterns that will release you from any negative stronghold in your life.

Whether you struggle with mental or spiritual conditions Pastor Sanabria acts as your guide as he teaches you how to overcome life's challenges.

"Conditions of The Heart" is a great read. The author incorporated his humor and wit into each and every lesson thought. I especially enjoyed the end of chapter exercises with reflection questions and memory verses; it is a genius way to incorporate instant applicability.

I highly recommend this book to anyone seeking a greater understanding of themselves and others when it comes to the complexities of the heart.

-Millie Perez, Author of: "Do You Love Me"
A romantic journey of self-discovery
and acceptance www.milliperez.com

Introduction

Have you ever been in an uncomfortable situation? Have you experienced things you would not wish on anyone else…not even your enemies? Have you ever made promises or internal covenants after going through life altering situations?

After making those promises, have you asked yourself these questions: "Why can't I get out of my situation? Why is it that I feel like everything I do turns out wrong? Why do I struggle while others have it all good?"

These are just a few but I am sure you have other questions similar to these. I have asked these questions many times over. And many times I came up short finding the answers. I have searched everywhere and in every place. One day I was even told, "Noel you are not where you should be." I questioned that as well. Not where I should be…where then should I be? These are questions that we ask ourselves after making these promises or internal covenants.

Internal covenants are promises made by us thinking that we will be protected by making them. We make them thinking they will be our security blankets. We believe it is the right thing to do. The issue is that when we are driven by impulse or emotion most times we make the wrong decision.

Conditions of the Heart will help you understand that most inner covenants or promises that we have made prevent us from being free and experiencing our God ordained purpose in this life. We struggle more and have health issues and relationship issues all because of those inner covenants. This book will help you by giving you several tools to break free and stay free. You will realize that the only way to experience success inwardly is by freeing yourself from those things that are hidden within your heart.

My desire is that once you are done with this book you can experience what I have experienced and be free just as I have been free. Not only become free but stay free! Then once you are done...pass it along to someone you know needs to be free.

Blessings!

Psalms 51:10 (LB)

"Create in me a new, clean heart, O God, filled with clean thoughts and right desires."

NOTES:

Chapter One

The Call

"Before I formed you I knew you, before you were born I set you apart; I appointed you…"
-Jeremiah 1:5 NIV

Every believers walk with Christ always begins with a call. Even before we make a decision to accept Christ as our Lord and Savior, He is calling us. Jeremiah 1:5 tells us; *"Before I formed you I knew you, before you were born I set you apart; I appointed you…" (NIV)* in other words, if He calls you it's because you were created by God for a certain purpose here on earth.

King Solomon tells us *"For everything there is a season, a time for every activity under heaven." (Ecclesiastes 3:1 NLT).*So whether it is to preach, teach, sing, own a business or drive trucks, there is a purpose. God places us in strategic areas in life because when HE calls us HE already has a plan for us.

Jesus called out to His disciples when He began His ministry here on earth. At one point He told Peter, *"follow Me and I'll make you fishers of men"*. That's a pretty intense decision for a fisherman to leave his life's work to follow some unknown, to walk into the unknown, to do something unknown.

We are not put on this earth by happen stance, but to serve God and to do the work of His Kingdom. The Lord said in Isaiah; *"I have called you back from the ends of the earth so you can serve me. For I have chosen you…"* (Isaiah 41:9 NLT) Now the important thing here is not to focus so much on the *'what'* you are called to do but on the simple fact that *'you are'* called to do something! We must remember that God does the calling and if He does the calling He will do the equipping and we in turn must do the seeking and the doing. The bible tells us many times to seek Him, to seek His wisdom, for all wisdom comes solely from God and we must be doers.

Far too many run from the calling of God as if that calling will not get a hold of them. My friend, it's like the old saying, 'you can run but you cannot hide' for *His word will not return to Him void!* So quit running. Fleeing is a strong sign of fear. And God does not give you a spirit of fear but of courage. To run can also show doubt and or even weakness. The Apostle Paul tells the Church that *"we are more than conquerors"* and John 4:4 declares *"greater is He that is within us."* Therefore there is no reason to fear if you trust in His Word!

The call of God may be overwhelming to some or even at the moment sound unbelievable and most times it's a call we may not have asked for. But be sure of this, if He calls you it is because He believes in you. If He appoints you, it's because He trusts in you. If He empowers you it's because He knows you can get the job done. God will gift you with whatever it is you will need for the specific task or tasks that He has placed in your life.

"There is always a beginning"

From Genesis to Revelation the Lord is calling all mankind. In Genesis chapter 3 He called out to Adam; *"Where are you?"* Not that God didn't know where Adam was…Adam needed to figure out where he himself was. In Exodus chapter 3 God calls Moses to deliver His people out of all things…a burning bush. In Samuel chapter 3 young Samuel is called. And if we read all the way at the end in Revelation chapter 3, Jesus says; *"I stand at the door and call"*. The question is; will you respond today to HIS call?

The Bible tells us of many great men who heard the call of God. As I already mentioned we know very well the story of little Samuel. Hannah, his mother, had prayed in the temple that if God would give her a child she would dedicate the child to God. Well, God answered her prayer and she had a son. When he was still young, Hannah took the child to the temple and presented him to Eli the priest.

3

The story continues where one night as Samuel was fast asleep he heard someone call his name. He thought it was old blind Eli calling so he went to him. Three times he heard his name being called and three times he asked Eli if he was calling him. The fourth time, Eli realized it must be the voice of God calling Samuel. The priest told young Samuel that the next time he hears the voice call his name to respond by saying, 'Speak Lord, I am listening'. From that moment on we know that Samuel played a significant part in choosing the first two kings of Israel – Saul and David.

In the New Testament we read about Philip. Jesus called Philip by saying, "Come with me". Philip races off and tells his brother Nathanael that the Messiah had called him to follow Him. Nathanael is not sold on the fact that Jesus was the Messiah so Philip invited him to "come and see". When Jesus spoke with Nathanael He explained that He knew Nathanael before they even met.

This turned Nathanael's skepticism into faith. Nathanael confessed "You are the Son of God! You are the King of Israel!" And, we know that these two men, Philip and Nathanael, became messengers of the Gospel.

Throughout time, we find God calling people to carry out specific tasks – wealthy and settled Abraham was called to leave everything and go to a land that God would show him. Again, the reluctant Moses was called to lead the people of Israel to freedom. The shepherd boy David, not old enough to shave, was called to be king. Gideon, who wanted proof that it was God who was really speaking to him, was called to lead an army against Israel's enemies. Jonah was called to carry a message of hope in Nineveh, a city he detested. Matthew, a cheat and a thief was called to be a disciple. Saul of Tarsus, the terrorist to the Christians, was called to be a missionary to the gentiles.

As you read the stories of these men and women who God had called, you may wonder if some of them, in fact, almost all of them would be our first choice. Jeremiah lacked confidence yet God called him to speak to God's enemies. When Mary was called to be the mother of our Savior, it seemed so wrong for so many reasons. She was too young, not married, too poor, too ordinary, but God called her just like that.

When Jesus called Peter, James and John, they were fishermen by trade with no other qualifications. Some even say they were rejects from the Synagogues. At times they seemed so dense and slow to catch what was being told to them, but God called them anyway.

What we find in each of these examples is that the people that God had called to do His work were ordinary people just like you and I – people with flaws and handicaps, people with their own issues and problems in their marriage or family, people that by human standards do not have much going for them. I read once that it is not beyond God to seemingly call the *wrong* people, for the *wrong* jobs at the *wrong* time and place. It may seem all wrong in our minds, but God knows what He is doing.

In all of these cases and in ours, God knows where we have lack, what skills we do not have and even the little to no confidence we possess. The call of God for their lives was going to test their confidence and commitment. And so, at the burning bush God told Moses, "I will be with you." Ex.3:12. To the doubt filled Gideon, God said, "Peace. Don't be afraid." (Judges 6:23). To young Jeremiah, God said, "Do not be afraid, I will protect you...I am giving you the words you must speak." (Jer 1:8-9). To Jonah He told him, "Go...and preach." (Jonah 1:2). And to His disciples Jesus last words were, "I will be with you always to the end of age." (Matt. 28:20).

God is the same yesterday today and forever – He does not change. He continues to do in us for us through us - what to us is crazy. He continues to call ordinary people just like you and me. His call will challenge us, confront us and test us. He still calls us to do His work here in this world because there are still far too many that need to hear the message of hope even though we, just like Jonah, may think they do not deserve it, or that we are the wrong people for Him to choose.

I remember when God called me. I was very young. It was a Tuesday night. But when He told me what He placed me on this earth for...I was speechless!

Here are some questions to reflect on:

What am I sensing God is asking me to do?

What is holding me back from walking in my calling?

Do I know my purpose on this earth?

Memory Scripture:

John 12:26

Whoever serves me must follow me; and where I am, my servant also will be.

My father will honor the one who serves me.

NOTES:

Chapter Two

The Resistance

9 But the Lord God called to the man, "Where are you?" 10 He answered,

"I heard you in the garden, and I was afraid because I was naked; so I hid."
Genesis 3:9-10 NIV

If we believe God is who He says He is and if we believe God wants only the best for us, then why do we resist His call to service? Jonah knew exactly what God wanted yet He resisted. The same holds true for many of us. God calls, most times we know what He wants and still we resist and refuse to obey and we run and hide – just like Adam did.

John 5 speaks of a man that had been sick for thirty eight years sitting by the pool called Bethesda. When Jesus saw him and asked him if he would like to be made well, and the Greek word for well is *Sozo*, which means to be restored, but the first thing this man did was give excuses.

> *"6 When Jesus saw him and knew he had been ill for a long time,*
>
> *he asked him, "Would you like to get well?" 7 "I can't, sir," the sick man said, "for I have no one to put me into the pool when the water bubbles up. Someone else always gets there ahead of me."*

There are far too many people that give God excuses and they themselves do not allow God to be God in their lives. At times we even make promises that bind us and prevent us from reaching our call or purpose in life. This happens all too often. "I can't", "I don't think I'm ready", "I am not educated enough" or "I will never do that again", "I will never let another man hurt me". We give excuses because either we are afraid of failing at something we have never tried or we are uncertain of the gifts and talents God has given us. Or perhaps it has something to do with our past.

The issue with this man was three fold; He was living in the wrong position, living with the wrong condition and expecting an easy transition! I'll explain. We cannot expect to move to a higher level in any area if we continue to hang with those things or people that keep us from, in George Jefferson's words, "Movin' On Up"! We need to re-position our lives and our minds so that God can operate how He desires to do so in and through our lives.

This man's condition was just as bad. Thirty eight years in the same condition is way too long. The bible tells us that of all the sick at that place *"Jesus looked at him and knew"*. In other words Jesus knew this man had been there for so long and something had to be done, not only physically but psychologically and emotionally as well. So Jesus asked the man; *"Do you want to be made whole?"*... but what was this man's response...excuses!

He used his past to try to explain the why's of his condition. God never asked this man about his past, yet he gave an entire history of why he was in that condition! In the same way Jesus approached this man He does with some us. It is not so much our physical conditions that Jesus wants to change as it is our mind. He wants to place things in order...He wants to restore us.

"What we think we become"

Paul the Apostle urges us to "be transformed by the renewing of your mind" (Romans 12:2) - why?

What we think we become. We cannot continue to focus on what happened but on what could be. This was Christ's intention with this lame man. He was trying to let this man know, before I work on the outside I need to first fix what's broke on the inside!

Jesus wanted to make this man understand that his condition was more affected by what he perceived of himself. If you think that you're traumatic experiences in previous relationships will happen in your next relationship you will always be bound to your perception. Proverbs 23:7 tells us that a man's innermost thoughts determine what he is. What a man thinks about himself will have a profound influence upon him.

The transition in this man's life occurred when he decided to believe and accept what Jesus was telling him. After he got up, he rolled up his mat and went off. What once carried this man is no more...now he is carrying his breakthrough!

"The School of Shepherds"

As I mentioned, I received my calling to ministry when I was fourteen years old. I remember it clearly. It was during a service dedicated to missions at my local church. I was sitting on the front church pew and a short elderly missionary from Guatemala called me to the front and began to tell me the story in John 21 of Jesus and Peter by the shore. After telling the story she touches my shoulders and say's; "God tells you today, 'Feed my sheep, for upon you is the calling to Pastor'".

And as I had also mentioned at the close of the last chapter, I was speechless. This really rocked my world - and not in a good way! Now, I am a Pastor's kid, and observing the things my parents went through while they were Pastor's really affected me. As I grew older I got involved in ministry in many areas. I was president of the youth ministry, became the youngest director of men's ministry, a translator, altar minister and Sunday school teacher. If there was a ministry in our church that I was able to get involved in I would.

That was all cool but there came a time in my life, as with most young men that I decided I wanted to get married. I met a beautiful young lady with whom I can say I am so in-love with still for more than 10 years. As we decided we wanted to get married, we sat with our pastor at that time for premarital classes. During these classes, there was a moment when he would ask about our family history. He asked how our relationship was with our parents. When it was my turn to speak about the relationship with my father, it's like I felt the temperature rise in that office and all I could simply say at that moment was, "I do not want to be like my father".

Now, this is not to say that my father was a bad man... on the contrary, he was a good man who loved God and I love him dearly. But, as I grew older I realized that I could not recount a day when my father had ever told me he loved me, not that he didn't, or gave me a hug or a kiss. Perhaps he did this when I was much younger, but never in my adolescence. This began to affect me as I matured. What I could remember is that my dad was busy being a Pastor.

There were times he would get home from his full time job to shower, change, and seldom had time to eat dinner, jumped in his car with all five of us kids plus my mother, drove about an hour to the church, hopped in the church van to pick up the church members. I am not even sure how many trips he made. He then had to open the church, turn on the heat, turn on the sound and then preach. I know you are probably tired already.

Once he was done preaching, he would greet everyone, most of those he greeted were going back in the same church van that he was going to drive them in! He then had to shut off the sound, the boiler, close the church, take the member's home, again, not sure how many trips. Then to drive back to the church, get the car and finally drive another hour or two back home to then look for parking in the neighborhood.

Now this went on several days during the week. So yea, this did have an effect on me. So what I did was make a vow, a *promise*, not to be like my father. Not in ministry and not in life. What a mistake. This is where my struggles within began.

Here are some questions to reflect on:

What or who am I allowing to grab hold of my attention?

What am I resisting?

Why do I struggle with staying the course?

Memory Scripture:

John 14:27 NLT

I am leaving you with a gift—peace of mind and heart. And the peace I give is a gift the world cannot give. So don't be troubled or afraid.

NOTES:

Chapter Three

Where Are You?

"'But the Lord God called to the man,
"Where are you?"'
Genesis 3:9 NIV

I did not understand that just years after God was dealing with me at that time. There was a point in my life, before I was married, that I decided to try and run from the call and ministry altogether, and begin a new life in, of all places, Puerto Rico.

The Sunday before flying out to Puerto Rico, I decided to go to my church and say my goodbye's to friends. Well, to my surprise God had a word for me. God told me; "who told you to make plans without consulting with me? I will allow you to travel but I will show you that I am your Lord." The next day I flew out to Puerto Rico.

For three months I tried to get work there and it became so difficult. I decided to call a family friend who is an evangelist and lived on the island and asked if I could stay with him for a few days and he said sure.

One night he had been invited to speak at a small church in a small town. As we ended the service and we were about to get into his car, an elderly lady with long white hair tugged on my sleeve and asked me; "What are you doing here? Go back to where you belong". This really freaked me out! It was as if God were asking; "Where are you?"

One Tuesday morning, after returning to my grandmother's house, one of my aunts from New York showed up. She always took some time to come to the island because she was soon going to be retired and was building her house. But as I reflect on this occasion, it was God ordained.

We began to talk when she asked me; "why are you here?" I told her that my intent was to start a new life in Puerto Rico. Her reply was; "this is not a place for you, you should go back home". I told her that I would like to but I had no money and no way of going back.

That evening I felt so broken and convicted. I fell to my knees and just began to cry all night. I began to talk with God and told him; "if You provide a way for me to go back home I promise to serve you with all my heart". That Thursday my aunt comes over the house again and she hands me an envelope. I asked what it was and she told me; "It's your ticket back home". She had bought me a first class ticket for me to go back home…I was blown away!

When I arrived back in New York I literally kissed the ground. From that moment on I decided to serve God with all my life…but there was still an issue! An issue I could not see and didn't know I had. Many times my Pastor would tell me; "Noel, you are not where you should be". This was something I struggled to understand. I thought I was seeking God and working in the ministry, but something kept me from reaching my calling and purpose.

Like many, I loved God, I served God but God was not first. "Seek ye first" is what scripture declares yet I was searching everything else first and God last.

I have understood over the years and in my walk with Christ that we have no idea what we need much less who we are. Take King David for example. He told the Lord to *"Search me, O God, and know my heart: try me, and know my thoughts."* Examine me, and see if I have not represented my feelings as they really are. You know me God, for you search me, and *"try my reins and my heart"*. What he was saying was "My desire is to be proved and tested".

Why? Because he understood that the heart is deceitful and that the ways of men are wicked. So he needed the Lord to search him. To examine his heart so David could know who he was through the Lord's eyes.

Ezekiel 36:26 (NIV) tells us; *"I will give you a new heart and put a new spirit within you; I will remove the heart of stone from your flesh and give you a heart of flesh"*.

God has a new heart for us that cannot be offended.

When a past offense or a hurt remain in our hearts, it causes serious spiritual consequences. Jesus speaks about this in Matthew 24:10-12 and mentions some of the dangers, such as: betrayal, hatred and cold love that grow on the inside as a result of holding on to those inner promises.

It can rob you of your peace and joy and replace it with insecurity because of fear. Just ask yourself, "Can I let my spouse go out with his or her friends alone without me calling or texting him or her every so often? Do I trust my spouse enough or do I need to keep tabs? This is a serious condition of fear and it is a result of comparing your present with your past. You are afraid that what happened in the past will repeat.

Our thoughts have a connection to our hearts. And it is not difficult to cite symptoms which show that the heart is not right. In order for your heart to be healed four things need to take place: Change your mind (repentance). Renew your mind, the mind is an outlet for the Spirit of God. Control your mind. The fact that the mind must be controlled is found in 2 Corinthians 10:5 when Paul commands "...bringing into captivity every thought to the obedience of Christ". And then there is occupy your mind. Here is what is written in Colossians 3:2 (RV) "Set your mind on the things that are above".

You have to learn to depend on God for it is God alone who can help you get rid of the past, rid of those insecurities and fears. Proverbs 1:33 NLT says; "But all who listen to me will live in peace, untroubled by fear of harm".

Here are some questions to reflect on:

Am I running from God?

Why am I running?

What is my greatest fear?

Memory Scripture:

Psalms 139:7

"I can never escape from your Spirit!
I can never get away from your presence!"

NOTES:

Chapter Four

What you can't see, can hurt you?

> *"No one lights a lamp and puts it in a place where it will be hidden, or under a bowl. Instead they put it on its stand, so that those who come in may see the light. 34 Your eye is the lamp of your body. When your eyes are healthy, your whole body also is full of light. But when they are unhealthy, your body also is full of darkness.*
>
> Luke 11:33 NIV

The subject of blindness is a very important subject in the Bible. All through Scripture, blindness is a spiritual metaphor. And it is used to represent the spiritual inability to see God's truth. As a man is physically blind, he cannot see God's *visible* revelation. That is he can't see the trees and the earth and the sky. But as a man is spiritually blind, he cannot see God's *invisible* revelation;

love, truth, holiness, forgiveness, blessing, eternal life, grace, joy, peace, etc.

As the blind does not see the vast blue of the clear sky, so the blind spirit does not see the vast holiness and purity of God. As the blind eye does not perceive the blanket of green that covers the earth, so the blind spirit cannot see the grace of God. As the blind eye does not see the immensity of creation, so the blind spirit does not see the limitless power of God. And as the blind eye sees no rainbow of colors that speckles the earth, so the blind spirit sees not the love of God which colors every revelation. As the blind eye cannot see light, so the blind spirit cannot see the light, the light of the world, Jesus Christ.

And so, blindness becomes scripturally a metaphor for spiritually being in the dark, unable to discern God or God's truth. And sadly but truly, spiritual blindness is the norm; spiritual sight, the exception.

Have you ever driven in a heavy rainstorm? Have you noticed that no matter how fast your wipers are running you still can't see clearly? Then, all of a sudden, as you are driving with as much caution as you can drive you run right into a huge pot hole in the road that messes your car up and messes you up! You had no idea it was there because the rain obstructed your view.

There are countless reasons as to why we become

blinded from seeing what is before us. The man at the pool of Bethesda had this issue. Though physically He saw Jesus, Spiritually he could not. He was asked if he wanted to be made well but could not see right away who was before him because he kept looking back. What are you looking at that is keeping you from seeing what or *who* is before you?

While looking for answers as to why I was not where I should have been, I realized I had no idea where I was. I could not see what that 'why' was! All I knew was that God wanted me back home and that He had a plan!

God often times allows us, in our journey to spiritual maturity, to confront certain issues that bring us to a breaking point in order for us to realize there is no other place for us to look but to Him. I guess that's why the Psalmist declared; *"I lift up my eyes to the mountains; where does my help come from? My help comes from the Lord, the Maker of heaven and earth."* There was no other place left to look but to God!

I was so lost in thinking that I was walking in the fullness of the calling placed over my life, that all was well, that I was doing the work of ministry but I was lost! I could not really see that I was in fact missing the mark. A very well-known Pastor once said; *"Just because you do well where you are does not mean that you are fulfilling God's purpose".* I believe God's purpose starts within us before it is manifested beyond us.

We can get lost in doing so well yet forget that we still need some good work done in us! The work of the Holy Spirit is never done in us. That is why he was sent - to be with us after Jesus' ascension. Jesus said, right before He left the earth; *"If you love Me, you will keep My commandments. I will ask the Father, and He will give you another Helper, that He may be with you forever; that is the Spirit of truth, whom the world cannot receive, because it does not see Him or know Him, but you know Him because He abides with you and will be in you."* John 14:14 (NASB)

The Holy Spirit dwells in us to help us by instructing us and guiding us, but we in our stinkin' human thinkin', wrap our minds with so many other things in our lives that we lose focus of Him. Many call it "burn out", which is a form of spiritual negligence.

This is when you want to help out in other areas in ministry or organizations, and at times you do well but fail to realize how much one begins to take on, that it gets to the point when your schedules are overbooked and then you begin to slowly butcher yourself. This can also happen in our personal lives. We begin to occupy our agendas trying to help everyone because if we don't we feel like we failed.

God did not call us to become overworked but to rest in Him, *to be still.* This is a common occurrence with so many. Perhaps you are reading this and you can relate to what I am saying. You need to chill out and take care of you! God wants to use you not abuse you my friend. He cannot use you if you are burnt out! We are needed not mistreated in the Kingdom!

I know, I know, you want to serve in everything you can and do for others. Get this in your mind…you cannot do everything for everyone! What you need to do is prioritize first. Set a plan out for your life whether you work in ministry, business or whatever it is. God is all about planning. He is an orderly God. He planned your life before the foundations of the world! Satan on the other hand is disorderly. Just read Genesis 1:2.

There was a time that ***I had become so caught up in the ministry that I allowed God to use me but did not allow Him to fix me.*** Sound familiar. I had plenty of speaking engagements, invites, outings, and I loved how God wanted to use me for His glory, yet I did not give Him time or space to work in me. My beautiful wife would also give me hints, and although I am not sure she even knew it, but God was using her so that I would not fall into that pit of self-abasement!

People don't usually stumble over boulders, they stumble over stones – relatively small things. When Jesus speaks about endurance, He is saying that it is easier to begin a race than finish it.

Between now and when you die, there will be major times of offense that you will need to overcome. We need to daily ask God for His help. We need to become people who are not ashamed to say, "Lord show me what needs to change in me." Becoming burnt out simply to avoid a fear or whatever it may be, is not the right way. You need to learn to make your past, your path to breakthrough.

Here are some questions to reflect on:

What do I really need to see?

What in my life is keeping me blind to the things of God?

What can I do to be free?

Memory Scripture:

2 Corinthians 4:4 NLT

> *Satan, who is the god of this world, has blinded the minds of those who don't believe. They are unable to see the glorious light of the Good News. They don't understand this message about the glory of Christ, who is the exact likeness of God.*

NOTES:

Chapter Five

It Must Happen From Within

"*Each one has to find his peace from within. And peace to be real must be unaffected by outside circumstances.*"
Mahatma Gandhi

Many times that is what holds us back from seeing what God wants us to see. Instead of looking out the windshield we keep looking at our rearview mirror. When we do this, we think our past is chasing us and it holds us back from reaching our full potential in Christ. Pastor Sergio De La Mora shares in his book that "*If we are not careful the voice of our past will cause us to slip back into those familiar patterns*" (Sergio De La Mora, The Heart Revolution[1], 2011, pg.22).

Your past could very well contain a number of issues that most had to or are currently dealing with. The freedom of Christ makes no exception of person. Today you can choose to be free! You may ask; "How?" Simple...the

Bible tells us; "You will know the truth, and the truth will set you free". Ok, then what is that truth? Jesus said; "I AM the <u>truth</u>". Once you encounter Jesus Christ you know the truth. And once you know the truth you will encounter freedom in Him, by Him, through Him! But in order for the Truth to be in you, you must learn to let go of the lie.

I remember Mark Batterson once said that at some point in our lives most of us stop living out of imagination and start living out of memory. That's the day we stop living and start dying. To be fully alive is to be fully present in the present. It mandates leaving the past in the past.

Paul said; *"I focus on this ONE thing: Forgetting the past and looking forward to what lies ahead, I press on…" (Philip.3:13,14a)* there are so many things that can influence our vision…so many distractions in life. We struggle with the flesh, the world and satan's attacks… but we must do as Paul did… "FOCUS ON THIS ONE THING: FORGET THE PAST AND LOOK FORWARD"!

Trust God that, *"When the enemy, (whatever it may be), comes in like a flood, the Spirit of the Lord shall lift up a standard against Him".* All you have to do is believe that God is able to deliver you out of your past and put you on track to your God ordained destiny. Believe me when I tell you He has an awesome plan for your life. Read what He said;

"This is God's Word on the subject: "I'll show up and take care of you as I promised and bring you back home. I know what I'm doing. I have it all planned out— plans to take care of you, not abandon you, plans to give you the future you hope for. When you call on me, when you come and pray to me, I'll listen. When you come looking for me, you'll find me. "Yes, when you get serious about finding me and want it more than anything else, I'll make sure you won't be disappointed." God's Decree. "I'll turn things around for you. I'll bring you back...bring you home...You can count on it."(Para-phrase mine) Jeremiah 29:10-12

When we allow God's Spirit to begin the work He desires in our hearts, an internal transformational explosion occurs. We not only know that the Spirit is working within us, but there is also a transferring of power to go from overcome to an overcomer, a victim to a victor. *"Behold! I have given you authority and power, and [physical and mental strength and ability] over all the power that the enemy [possesses]; and nothing shall in any way harm you." (Luke 10:19 AMP)* Gods plan includes the indwelling power, *dunamis*, of His Holy Spirit. We can be assured He will be with us always.

We all want to move forward. We all have a past. But in order to move forward we have to let the past stay just there...in the past.

I remember when I first began driving. I was anxious and nervous. I remember I used to have one foot on the brakes and one foot on the gas pedal. As I accelerated on the gas pedal I still had my left foot on the brake pedal. This had caused acceleration but did not allow the car to move. When I released the brake pedal the car took off. I was so scared after that event.

This is how many people live when they do not let go of the past. We have the desire and the want but refuse to let go of the brake pedal. Mary Manin Morrissey quoted; *"Even though you may want to move forward in your life, you may have one foot on the brakes. In order to be free, we must learn how to let go. Release the hurt. Release the fear. Refuse to entertain your old pain. The energy it takes to hang onto the past is holding you back from a new life".*

Jesus was no exception from temptations or trials. But each time He overcame. He showed us that we too can overcome. God can walk with you in your fiery furnace. He can be firm with you in your Lion's den. He will stand with you in the storm, be present in your Gethsemane and faithful in your Jericho. All you need to do is trust.

Someone once said; "Yesterday is not ours to recover, but tomorrow is ours to win or lose". This quote sounds familiar: *"I have set before you life and death, the blessings and the curses; therefore choose life, that you and your descendants may live".* Deuteronomy 30:19 (NKJV) It is interesting to note that it says "choose life, that you and your descendants shall live". What you decide to do from this point on not only has an eternal impact on your own life but also on your children and your children's children. You can leave a legacy of curses or you can leave a legacy of breakthrough and freedom! It can start now and it can start with you!

A good friend of mine shared her story which relates to what I am conveying. I will call her Isy for privacy. Here is Isy's heart condition and how God stepped in and began to create a new heart.

"In the month of April of 1979 God granted me the privilege to enter into this world. I was born and raised in a Christian home where I learned about the gospel and walked in the ways of the Lord.

At the age of fifteen I began to detract from the very teachings they taught in my home. I became what they call a backslider. I had I began to live as a disobedient teenager where I would often lie simply to get whatever I wanted no matter who was involved.

I remember that in a youth service I had gone to, I had met this young boy who was serving the Lord and had caught my attention with his look. My parents were totally against this relationship for one he was much older than me. Since I thought I knew it all and in spite of my parents not agreeing with it, I decided to continue with the relationship which began as a respectful and caring relationship until sometime after it became more obsessive in which the young man did not want me speaking to any friends or going to any youth events because this young man thought that I would become unfaithful to him.

There came a time when we would see each other secretly in the early mornings so that my parents would not find out about us. But it came to a point that this young man began to physically hit me on several occasions.

I remember that my mother and my sister would ask what happened to me each time they saw marks on my body. But not to get the young man in trouble I would say that I had fallen or that I banged into the door of the car or whatever excuse I could muster up in order to protect the boy. Every time this boy would physically harm me he would tell me it was not his intention to do it and that I provoked him because of certain comments I would make and that as a child he was also abused by his father and that is why he would lose his temper and take it out on me.

Now, at the age of seventeen, we committed a sinful act and I became pregnant by the young man. To my surprise the young man decided not to be involved because he was not ready to take on the responsibility that comes with having a child.

During my pregnancy, I also experienced rejection from many family members because they did not think it was right for someone so young to raise a child much less have one. I remember some telling me that that child I was going to have would amount to nothing and had no promising future and that I had nothing to offer him. Despite all the criticism and rejection that I received, I decided to go on with my pregnancy.

On one early morning in August, my beautiful baby boy was born. As you could imagine, having a child at such a young age is nothing easy, but I thank God that my mother and father were always there for me and helped me raise my boy.

Once my son was born, I became very arrogant, prideful and vain. I would spend lots of time in dance clubs and very attracted to the desires of the world. I thought I had everything I needed but each time the weekend would end I would once again feel empty and frivolous.

I remember on one occasion during a conversation with my mother, she had suggested it would be good for me to go visit my older sister in the United States, which I hadn't seen in six years. So I decided to take that trip.

In January of 2000 I arrived to Pennsylvania. Now my plans were to visit my sister for seven days and then go back home to Puerto Rico. Seven days had gone by and I decided to stay in Pennsylvania with my son to begin a new life.

Today it has been thirteen years since making that trip from my home across seas to Pennsylvania. During these years, I surrendered my heart to God and the Lord has shown me His grace in great ways. Here is where I met my new husband, who has been a father figure and role model for my son and an amazing husband.

In July of 2010 I was invited by a coworker to attend a service at her church, and that day I publicly turned my life to the Lord. I have been attending this church for a little over three years and I must say that the change in my personal life and in the life of my family has been nothing short of amazing.

God has been so good and faithful that my son is now part of the worship band in the church, I sing on the worship team and my husband is part of the technical team. And in July of 2013 I had the awesome privilege to be a part of the mission's team, a medical group that travels constantly to Haiti.

God has done many changes in my life personally and spiritually as well in my family that I had thought was impossible, but I realized that for God nothing is impossible. I now consider myself a young woman that is loving and caring, one who loves to serve and above all that has an unconditional love for God.

I know that in the same way that God has renewed my heart and transformed my life and my family, He can easily do it for you today. All you have to do is trust Him. If you trust Him He will show you the path you need to take. From personal experience I can say that He never fails. I serve a God that is true to His Word."

You must choose to find the strength that God has given you within in order to begin the change you crave for!

Questions to reflect on:

What do I need to let go of in order to walk into God's plan for my life?

When I compare what I will gain in Christ to what I will lose from the world, is it worth it?

Where do I think is a good place to start?

Memory Scripture:

Romans 12:1 NLT

> *And so, dear brothers and sisters, I plead with you to give your bodies to God because of all he has done for you. Let them be a living and holy sacrifice, the kind he will find acceptable.*
>
> *This is truly the way to worship him.*

NOTES:

Chapter Six

Mind Monsters

*"You keep him in perfect peace whose mind
is stayed on you, because he trusts in you."*
Isaiah 26:3 ESV

I once read the following statement; "the mind is a special gift from God. It can potentially store 100 trillion thoughts. And it is a tool that God wants to use in your life to fulfill His purposes. Yet there are a lot of people fighting for access to that mind of yours." If it is so, then we have to be on our guard. The battlefield of life begins in the mind. If you can change your mind you can change your heart.

Paul exhorts us to *"take every thought captive and make it obey Christ."* (2 Corinthians 10:5 GNB) What does this mean? It means there will be opinions and then thoughts of insecurities, suicide, confusion, anxiety and even rebellion – but we must put those thoughts and opinions captive to the truth of who God is and trust what He is capable of doing in, through and for our lives!

Now look how awesome is our God. Paul tells us; *"all glory to God, who is able, through his mighty power at work within us, to accomplish infinitely more than we might ask or think."* In other words, any thought that we may have or receive cannot compare to the thoughts God already has towards us – and His thoughts can do so much more beyond what we can ever think or imagine.

"I don't think the way you think. The way you work isn't the way I work." God's Decree. "For as the sky soars high above earth, so the way I work surpasses the way you work, and the way I think is beyond the way you think. Just as rain and snow descend from the skies and don't go back until they've watered the earth, Doing their work of making things grow and blossom, producing seed for farmers and food for the hungry, So will the words that come out of my mouth not come back empty-handed. They'll do the work I sent them to do, they'll complete the assignment I gave them" (Isaiah 55:8 MSG).

We need to allow Gods plan to take form in our lives. But the mind monsters will not stop coming. What can you do? Guard yourself. Put on what the Bible calls "The Helmet of Truth". Fill your mind with the Truth, the Word of God.

Whenever doubt, the flesh, or simply a negative

thought comes to try and invade your mind, remember what Jesus used against the devil when he was tempted in the desert – "IT IS WRITTEN".

Correct thinking always leads to correct action. Someone once shared that whatever is above our heads is always beneath His feet. And many times as believers, we tend to run from the very things we have power over.

What we do, many times, is listen to and surrender to these messages that they have taken root in our hearts and become the words by which we live.   Do not entertain them and do not give negative thoughts the authority over your mind. They can drain you spiritually, emotionally, psychologically and physically.

I was once a victim myself to these voices and thoughts. Few people, if any, knew the dissatisfaction I felt toward myself growing up. I always appeared as a self-assured young man. I was guarding or hiding what I really felt by going places and keeping busy.

See, if you don't learn to separate what you do from who you are, when you fail at what you do, it will make you feel that you also failed at who you are because often we mistake what we do for who we are. Function and identity are two distinct ideas.

If you already find yourself struggling with these *mind monsters*, and have gotten exhausted along the way… know that Jesus does not want to leave you in that condition. He tells you today; *"Are you tired? Worn out? Burned out…? Come to me. Get away with me and you'll recover… I'll show you how to take a real rest. Walk with me… watch how I do it. I won't lay anything heavy or ill-fitting on you. Keep company with me and you'll learn to live freely and lightly" (Matthew 11:28-30 MSG Para-phrase mine).*

If a man thinks right, he will be right. If he thinks wrong, he will be wrong. If he thinks nothing, he will be nothing. As Emerson stated it "A man is what he thinks about all day long." The Word of God tell us that man's innermost thoughts determine what he is (Proverbs 23:7; Para-phrase mine).

If you have surrendered to these thoughts and you have given up, I encourage you to get back up. If you are thinking of giving up, I also encourage you to keep on keepin' on! You're almost there.

Do not allow your past or those promises you have bound yourself to keep you from breaking free and experiencing your next level of glory. There is nothing impossible for my God. What to man seems impossible God says, "I got this". You are not what your past was!

Remember friends, our present circumstances will have an effect in us, whether positively or negatively, it depends solely on how we allow them to impact us. But there is great news; every problem has an expiration date! Examine for a moment what Paul said; *"For I consider that the sufferings of this present time (this present life) are not worth being compared with the glory that is about to be revealed to us and in us and for us and conferred on us!" (Rom.8:18 AMP).* Hallelujah!

As I mentioned before, God loves us so much that He does not want to leave us in the condition that He finds us in. He wants you and me both to experience Him and be transformed from glory to glory! In order for this to happen we must keep our hearts available to Him because at any moment a God transition can occur and you cannot miss God in the transition.

You have a choice. Perry Noble wrote, "Change begins with a decision." (Overwhelmed book). What do you choose? Do you wish to continue to be overcome or do want to overcome? Your circumstance will always remain the same until you decide to change it!

Philip Yancey wrote, "For many people, it takes the jolt of tragedy, illness, or death to create an existential crisis of faith. At such a moment, we want clarity; God want our trust."

Sergio De La Mora also shared that "adversity is the raw material of great faith." Also, "God uses adversity to focus your thoughts and attention to Him."

So my challenge to you is simple, let it go! Whatever they did… whatever they said… do yourself a favor, and let it go! If you don't, you will continue to torment your soul and you will not be able to move forward to the greater days ahead. Use what you have gone through as a tool to 1) put your focus and trust in God, 2) help others to trust in God, 2) share with others how God brought you through.

Do as Jesus did, memorize scripture so that when these mind monsters try to attack... you have weapons to fight them off. The only way to guard your mind is by guarding your heart!!!

Stay focused!

Questions to reflect on:

1. What mind monsters are currently tormenting my thoughts?

2. Have I surrendered to these negative thoughts?

3. Are those around me a good influence or a negative influence?

Memory Scripture:

Luke 6:45 NLT

"A good person produces good things from the treasury of a good heart, and an evil person produces evil things from the treasury of an evil heart. What you say flows from what is in your heart."

NOTES:

Chapter Seven

Moving Forward

"The course of a person's life will always be determined by the condition of their heart".

~Sergio De La Mora

What is it that is stopping you from moving forward? What is that thing…that hurt…that past experience that you are holding on to? You don't think about it but you haven't let it go. You must take the breaks off in order for your life to move forward. So what is it?

Sometimes, we need to simply sing out loud; I'm not going back, I'm moving ahead, Here to declare to You (Jesus) my past is over in You, All things are made new, surrendered my life to Christ, I'm moving forward. What this declaration is telling us is that the only way to move forward is through a surrendered life to Christ. I can tell you this is true because I have experienced this. Only God can make a way where in our eyes and in our minds there doesn't seem to be a way.

Your heavenly Father designed your spirit, soul and body. He ordains and oversees their alignment. My prayer and hope is that His Holy Spirit will speak to your spirit the truth that you are created by Him...affirmed by Him...capable...and beloved in Him. That He has no lack...no limit. Nothing can separate you from His love. God liked the way He created you. When God created you He said you were good. God is perfectly sure of His ability to heal those areas, to restore the broken places and hurting areas.

My desire is that you can live free from the spirit of fear that would paralyze you...fears for the future, fears of failure, fears of meaninglessness, and fears of man. You can live in hope, peace and with great joy. God's promises are Yes and Amen for your life. He wants to put in order what has become disorderly in your life. He does not desire for you to walk into your future with the same baggage of yesterday.

If you can learn to look at your issues of the past... the hurts of yesterday as stepping stones towards your breakthrough instead of stumbling blocks, I believe your life will change for the better. Proverbs 3:5-6 gives us this wisdom; *"Trust in the Lord will ALL your heart, and DO NOT lean on YOUR own understanding. In ALL your ways ACKNOWLEDGE HIM, and HE WILL make straight your paths."* (ESV) And Isaiah gives this advice *"Remember not the former things, nor consider the things of old."* Isaiah 43:18 ESV.

The Lord told David *"I will instruct you and teach you in the way you should go; I will counsel you with my eye upon you"* (Psalm 32:8 ESV). The problem is that we choose to go our own ways and do things the way we are comfortable with. But that is how we end up the way we are. That is the way to become frustrated and we put the blame on people and situations and circumstances. Consider Solomon's teaching on this subject; *"There is a way that seems right to a person, but its end is the way that leads to death."*

You can move forward in victory. You can move forward into a new level. You can move forward and have breakthrough. Whatever your struggle...whatever your past...whatever the hurt...God is the same...He changes not! You can break down the walls that are hindering you from seeing and experiencing all that God has for you. You can walk in the freedom of knowing that your past is no longer weighing you down. That the hurts of the past is not a pathway to hatred & bitterness but a stepping stone to reaching new dimensions of glory in Jesus.

The Bible speaks of those who try to make their own path. Those who search in every other place but in Jesus. *"The way of a fool is right in his own eyes, but a wise man is he who listens to counsel"* (Proverbs 12:15 NASB). We need to think clearly. When we carry too much clutter our thoughts are obscured and we cannot think right. We become like fools. God said we are wise when we seek advice…counsel.

In Genesis we read the story of Abram and his nephew Lot. They had pitched their tents between a place called Bethel and Ai. During this time Abram had a lot of livestock and Lot was also carrying with a lot of livestock. They each had their family and servants with them. Some fighting began between both sides and Abram told Lot they would have to separate to avoid the fighting because where they were there was not enough land to contain both sides.

After Lot chose which direction he would travel, God showed up and told Abram what He was going to give him. We pick up the story in chapter 13 verses 14-17 of Genesis;

"After Lot had gone, the Lord said to Abram, "Look as far as you can see in every direction – north, south, east and west. I am giving all this land, as far as you can see, to you and your descendants as a permanent possession. And I will give you so many descendants that, like the dust of the earth, they cannot be counted! GO and WALK through the land in every direction, for I am giving it to you." (NLT)

Now, notice that God Himself was telling Abram that He was "giving" him all of that land and all of those descendants. But even though God was giving it to Abram, God still commanded Abram to do something in order to receive what he was being given…God told Abram to "GO and WALK". Today God tells you the same but in different words… "LET IT GO and GIVE IT UP". He wants what you really don't need…the hurts, the past, and the fears.

You have tried for so long to escape your pains, your hurts, and your past but to no avail. You have tried hiding it as if it would not show again. You have tried forgetting it but then something is triggered and it reminds you of that experience or that person or that moment. It could be a place you went, a picture, a thought, someone who resembles your abuser or accuser. It is not a good feeling. You try hard to get it out of your mind but it is there and it is haunting you. It only follows you because you have not let it go. Choose to be free today…right now!

I read a story of one lady that had been abused from childhood both emotionally and physical. She stated that she had no idea how her future would be affected. If Satan can convince us that we're worthless, he can immobilize us and keep us from fulfilling God's plan for our lives.

When not confronted the results are devastating. Most of the time we are so lost in the pain that we cannot overcome the hurt. However, a life of abuse, rejection, bitterness and hate can be turned around. Though you walk through the storms, Jesus can and will hold the waters and the winds steady. You can find freedom in the present when you allow Jesus to heal you from your past.

Keep moving forward!

Questions to reflect on:

What roadblock have I allowed along the way?

How difficult is it for me to remove these road blocks?

What can I do to forget what is behind me and continue to move forward?

Memory Scripture:

Philippians 3:13-14 NLT

> *13 No, dear brothers and sisters, I have not achieved it, but I focus on this one thing: Forgetting the past and looking forward to what lies ahead, 14 I press on to reach the end of the race and receive the heavenly prize for which God, through Christ Jesus, is calling us.*

NOTES:

Chapter Eight

Transitions

"Change is the essence of life. Be willing to surrender what you are for what you could become"

Reinhold Neibuhr

During the time when my wife and I lived in NY, she had asked me a question that caused me to say; "Hugh" - In a Scooby Doo voice. She asked, what did I think about moving to Pennsylvania? Without a thought I said NO! Well, honestly it was more graphic than that but we will stick with the simple No!

At the time I did not realize that God was already setting us up. See, God has a blue print regarding your life. God says; "I know what I'm doing. I have it all planned out – plans to take care of you, not abandon you, plans to give you the future you hope for." Jeremiah 29:11 MSG

I learned that transition defined is, "The act of passing

from one state or place to the next," or "an event that results in transformation." That's pretty deep. You can be certain of one thing; <u>transition does not allow you to stay in the same place</u>. You can fight it all you want, but it will let you know, "I am here," and until you transition to the expected state, you and I will continue to struggle within ourselves.

Throughout Jesus' ministry, transitioning people from one state to another was His goal, whether it was in thoughts, deeds, in health, and in speech. However, more often than not, the people missed the moment.

Jesus told a certain rich young ruler; *"If you want to be complete, go, sell what you own, and give the money to the poor. Then you will have treasure in heaven. And come follow me." Matthew 19:21 CEV* The young rulers response was surprising. *"22But when the young man heard this, he went away saddened, because he had many possessions." Matthew 19:22CEV*

This young ruler, though, missed the transition moment because he focused on his property, instead of what Jesus was offering. Now how could this young ruler be mad at Jesus, the giver of life, when He, the *GIVER*, was offering the very life this young ruler desired? It is easy to ask this question when we are on this outside looking in, but we are all guilty of missing God in transition moments.

I learned of these three reasons as to why we miss God in these transition moments.

- **The picture is not clear.** Most times when we approach God, we want Him to give us a clear picture of what our lives should be [Before I relocate, I need to know where I will work, how much I will make, and where I will live, etc.]. There is nothing wrong with this expectation, except God tells us to *"Go and I will show you,"* *(Genesis 12:1)* and not a land I *have* shown you. *"Follow me and I will make you fishers of men,"* *(Matthew 4:19)*, it's not because I have made you fishers of men. The picture always becomes clearer when we follow Him.

- **The assignment is too daunting.** It is interesting how the Bible describes the rich young ruler. First, he is rich, he is young, and he is a ruler. To transition this man, Jesus reaches to the very core of his identity: to give it all up! Yes, he could have given it up, but would he have risked being poor and not rule, at the expense of his reputation? This command from Jesus to this young ruler was too daunting, hence he settled; when he was supposed to have his moment of transition.

- **The timing is not right.** Dr. Samuel Chand said; "When you are 100% sure, you are too late." We have an approach to life with the attitude of, "it needs to feel right" before I can make the change. However, I am yet to come across a situation in my life or in the Word where the timing felt 100% right. *"In His time, He makes all things beautiful,"* *(Ecclesiastes 3:11),* not our time. When those who wanted to follow Jesus needed more time to finish off personal business, Jesus had this to say, *"No one, after putting his hand to the plow and looking back is fit for the Kingdom of God."*

I am sure there are other reasons as to why we miss out on those moments of God transitions that He desires us to experience. Perhaps it's lack of trust, lack of faith, fear of the unknown, and the list is endless. But is it really worth it to miss God in these transition moments for our lives because of our own insecurities and lack of trust in Him?

I believe it is worth the risk. When my wife asked me about moving to Pennsylvania my first response was no way. But as the years passed she asked the same question again in 2006 and my response was different – I said yes. This decision was our moment of transition and transformation as a family and a ministry. I had no reason to continue where we were. I had a feeling in my gut that something huge was in the works but didn't know what.

We learn three key points about obedience from the story of Abraham and his son Isaac.

1. Our level of obedience should always be greater than our sacrifice.

2. Obedience is an act of worship.

3. Obedience is the path that leads to provision.

God is always up to something. Always on the move always preparing. And when we obey we begin to see what He has planned for us.

A friend of ours at church, shared about how God surprises us. He stated; "They told him, "Joseph is still alive! In fact, he is ruler of all Egypt." Jacob was stunned; he did not believe them. —Genesis 45:26

The news to Jacob was unexpected. God loves to do things like that. Sometimes He plans and prepares for a long time. He waited thousands of years before He finally sent His Son into the world. Yet sometimes God likes to do something so suddenly that no one is quite prepared for it. For Jacob, the news that Joseph was alive was stunning. He fainted (according to the King James Version).

The news about Joseph surpassed anything Jacob had ever expected. If you were to ask Jacob what was his wildest dream, he would not have named what his sons told him. He had already concluded that Joseph was dead—that he was out of the picture. I wonder if you have already reached conclusions about which you are so certain that you are unable to conceive any alternative situation.

The wonderful thing was the news that Joseph was alive, but then to learn that he was the lord of all Egypt was almost inconceivable. God loves to do that. He loves to do that which surpasses anything that we ever thought of. When the queen of Sheba came to Solomon, she said, "I had heard of your fame, I had heard of your wisdom, I had heard of your riches. Having seen it, even the half had not been told to me." (See 1 Kings 10:7.)

The apostle Paul said that when we pray, God does that which goes beyond what we ask for or even think about. "No eye has seen, no ear has heard, no mind has conceived what God has prepared for those who love him" (1 Cor. 2:9). God has a plan for every single one of us. When we see what He has in mind, it will surpass anything we thought possible. He wants to give us the desires of our hearts beyond anything we thought possible.

See, I say it again, God was up to something but I had no idea what it was. I knew there was something brewing but I never knew I needed some work done within my heart first.

Some points to reflect on:

Here is a list of the symptoms of spiritual heart disease:

(Check all that apply)

Do I have a:

- Blocked faith

- Fear

- Inability to understand spiritual principles or events

- Exclusive focus on the physical realm. Looking only for physical solutions.

- Unbelief, Inability to see God

- Inability to believe in and trust the word of God

Memory Scripture:

Psalms 51:16-17 NLT

16 You do not desire a sacrifice, or I would offer one. You do not want a burnt offering.

17 The sacrifice you desire is a broken spirit.

You will not reject a broken and repentant heart, O God.

NOTES:

Chapter Nine

Why Am I Here?

*"And we know that for those who love God
all things work together for good,*

*for those who are called according to His
purpose"*

Romans 8:28 ESV

The most basic question asked is "What on earth am I here for? What's my purpose?" A great question to ask. In his book "What on earth am I here for?" Pastor Rick Warren[2] writes about a certain philosophy professor at Northeastern Illinois University, who once wrote to 250 of the best-known philosophers, scientists, writers, and intellectuals in the world, asking them, "What is the meaning of life?" Like many they began to search for the answer but all they had were speculations. Pastor Rick shares that there is an alternative to speculation and that is revelation.

Albert Einstein quoted *"Only a life lived for others*

is a life worthwhile." But it is difficult to live for others when you can no longer trust anyone because you think that if you open your heart to others they too will hurt you or abuse you or cause pain. These are defenses we build because of the issues we have been through and yes we do not want to go through them again.

God's plan for your life does not include being secluded… lonely… hurt… in pain… depression… or having distrust. We need God to deal on the inside in order for us to live free and do good not only for but unto others. We need His revelation.

God's design is for us to serve…help…love one another…that includes "EVERYONE". And Paul tells us that *"It's in Christ that we find out who we are and what we are living for. Long before we first heard of Christ …he had his eye on us, had designs on us for glorious living, part of the overall purpose he is working out in everything and everyone."* Ephesians 1:11 (MSG)

When we moved to Pennsylvania in May of 2006, we placed several signs before the Lord. Everything was going well and we truly believed that God used those signs to simply get us to where we are today. One thing I did know, I was moving to unfamiliar territory.

Unbeknownst to me, God was setting us up. He was orchestrating everything as I allowed Him to. As humans, our thinking is rational and practical and our perspective is short, but God has a plan that to us is so far out there. For us something may be a great idea but what God has planned is always beyond great. *"No eye has seen, no ear has heard, and no mind has imagined what God has prepared for those who love him."* 1 Corinthians 2:9.

The fact is that when we allow God to work in us, He will transition that work through us and use it for us. There is no doubt about that. "All things work together for the good." I simply trusted God to lead us to make our crooked paths (our minds) straight. We could not depend on rationale or on simply skill; we needed the guidance of His Spirit.

There were times where we have tried doing things on our own, oh they lasted for a while but then it would turn out to be a struggle. Why, Because God did not have His hand on it. So, I would say we learned our lesson. We learned to depend on God, and during this time, when we were unfamiliar to where we had moved to, we truly needed to trust Him.

When we had decided we were going to move I sat with my Pastor and shared my heart about moving. I told him I did not hear God's voice but that everything I learned regarding faith, trust, and being led by the Spirit needed to be put into action. So we moved to unfamiliar territory.

During our time of prayer and planning, the story of Abraham came up. As I searched the scripture about his journey I noticed what God told him; *"The LORD said to Abram, "Leave your land, your relatives, and your father's home. Go to the land that I will show you."* Genesis 12:1 (CEB)

Notice what God told Abram; "Leave your land, your relatives, and your father's home." In other words, God was telling him, "Leave what you are familiar with, what you are used to, what you are comfortable with and TRUST Me." This is something God tells us when He calls us. Because what He has planned is far better than what we can think or imagine.

This is where many times we fail. Where we come up short. Where we rob ourselves from what God wants to give us. We struggle with trusting His plan and purpose because of the simple fact that we cannot see therefore we are not so secure. Pastor Sergio De La Mora also shared in his book The Heart Revolution: "A relationship with Jesus will always lead to an 'I can' on the inside of you".

For me this means there will be a change in attitude. A change in thought. When this occurs we begin to develop the mind of Christ that Paul speaks of in Philippians 2:5. Pastor Sergio continues to share this thought; "God is not interested in measuring our mistakes and successes; He just wants to know if we'll believe in Him and stay connected to Him through a genuine personal relationship with His Son."

So what should our response be? Simple… to trust in the Lord God! I believe that God tells us the same thing He told Joshua; *"Be strong, vigorous, and very courageous. Be not afraid, neither be dismayed, for the Lord your God is with you wherever you go."* Joshua 1:9b. AMP. So if that's all it takes then why do we struggle with it? So whatever the reason is, just trust. Trust in the Creator of the universe. Trust in the Great I AM. Trust in THE WAY, THE TRUTH, THE LIFE… no other but Jesus! Jesus promised never to leave us nor forsake us. If He said it He will do it!

Jesus shares a few Parables or stories in the 15th chapter of the book of Luke. What Jesus was trying to say was that no matter how deep the pit or dark the night, He will always look for you and rescue you because He loves you with an everlasting love according to Jeremiah 31:3.

Now I want to challenge you to look closely and understand these words… *I love you with an EVERLASTING LOVE*. What God wants you to know is that His love has no beginning and has no due date. No matter how much you've messed up, He still loves you!

God is communicating to you that you cannot mess up enough to get rid of His love for you. How about that? It is safe to say that to Him you are precious.

Simply imagine what the outcome would be if we simply left our past…our fears in the hands of The Creator.

He knows what is good and what we need. There is no evil in Him, no mistakes in Him, no abuse. But yes there is Joy, Love, Peace and comfort. But you must be willing to leave it in His hands.

Here's a thought:

It All Starts with God!

COLOSSIANS 1:16 (NLT) *"for through him God created everything in the heavenly realms and on earth. He made the things we can see and the things we can't see—such as thrones, kingdoms, rulers, and authorities in the unseen world. Everything was created through him and for him."*

It's not about you. The purpose of your life is far greater than anything you can imagine. If you don't know why you are here, I'll tell you… It's all about God. You were born by his purpose and for his purpose. Just check out what Romans 11:36 (NLT) says; "For from him and through him and for him are all things. To him be the glory forever! Amen."

NOTES:

Chapter Ten

Heart Conditions

"Because God has made us for Himself, our hearts are restless until they rest in Him."

Augustine of Hippo

What is the heart or soul?

Hebrews 12:1 tells us, *"let us strip off every weight that slows us down, especially the sin that so easily trips us up. And let us run with endurance the race God has set before us."* Many people are trying to run this race with so much weight in their hearts. Carrying all that weight will cause us to faint and stumble. When your heart fails and stumbles it fails because of fear. Scripture tells us that *"men's hearts will fail because of fear"* Luke 21:26. I once heard someone say, "It is ok to look at the world around us but you do not need to pay attention to it." That's interesting because look at what Isaiah said;

> 3*"You will keep in perfect peace all who
> trust in you, all whose thoughts are fixed
> on you!*
>
> 4*Trust in the Lord always, for the Lord God
> is the eternal Rock." Is.26:3-4*

What we should be doing is focusing on Jesus. If we want to keep our hearts healthy we need to focus our attention on something healthy. *"Whom have I in heaven but You? And besides You, I desire nothing on earth. My flesh and my heart may fail; But God is the strength of my heart and my portion forever."(Ps.73:25-26 NLT)*

Notice that David say's "My flesh (health) and my heart (soul) may fail." I once heard a pastor say that no flesh ever failed on its own. "Out of the abundance of the heart speaks the mouth". Keep your heart healthy! This is why Paul always exhorted the church to Guard their hearts. And we need to understand that we are not the strength of our heart...NO... according to David...God is!

Pastor Perry Noble once said; "If you don't let your past die, it won't let you live." Powerful! What truth does this have regarding our heart? Our past is the weight we continue to carry into our future.

We have our past hurts and our past secrets that we want no one to know about because it is shameful or embarrassing, past abuse, past relationships, past failures, and we think if we keep all of this baggage shut up in our hearts eventually we will be ok. But I want to tell you right now, the only way you will experience freedom is by giving that area of your heart to Jesus who created that heart without all the weight. He did not create your heart to be a closet cluttered with shame, hurt, abuse or any other thing that would keep Him out. He wants to fill you with His love and His hope and His peace.

King David wrote; "I am sick at heart. How long, O Lord, until you restore me?" (Psalms 6:3 NLT) As King, as the anointed King that God Himself handpicked, he knew he needed healing in his heart. This is a man who at this time has had a lot of success... a lot of wealth... a lot of possessions... but he was sick in his heart. And he knew this.

This sickness in the heart can cause many things to happen some of which David himself begins to describe in verse 6; "I am worn out from sobbing. All night I flood my bed with weeping, my vision is blurred by grief; my eyes are worn out because of all my enemies."

Notice what happened? First he says he is worn out because of the sorrow the pain is causing. He fills his pillows with tears. In other words he cannot sleep well. He also shares how he cannot see right...not only are his eyes heavy from lack of sleep, his vision is beginning to diminish.

Many have a misconception when it comes to opening

that area of their heart. Their thinking is that if they open that area they will continue to be haunted. But it's quite the opposite that will happen. As David describes in the following two verses, "Go away, all you who do evil, for the Lord has heard my weeping. The Lord has heard my plea; the Lord will answer my prayer".

God will take our past hurts and begin to heal and set us free. Like the TV show "house crashers", God will come in with His team, The Father The Son and The Holy Spirit (John 14:23) and begin a NEW renovation in your heart. All you need to do is give Him your heart and allow Him to begin the process.

Adam had this heart issue. He was created with a perfect heart. He lived perfect. He was in perfect peace. Perfect love up until, like the old saying; he put his foot where his mouth was. Once he fell into the game of deceit God came asking for him. Adam answered by saying; *"I heard you walking in the garden, and I was afraid because I was naked so I hid"*. Genesis 3:10.

He was free of shame before the fall. He was free of guilt before the fall. He was free of burden before the fall. But after the fall he became burdened, shameful and felt the weight of guilt. This is another tactic the enemy uses to make us feel guilty and burdened and ashamed... something God never intended for us to have.

A good friend of mine who is also a Pastor shared her

story with me regarding The Condition of her Heart. To protect her identity I will call her Mary.

Mary shared that when she was a little girl she said she would never marry a pastor let alone become one. And if you really think about it, she didn't. She married a wonderful man who loves the Lord. One of her passions is training. She really enjoys helping in the field of non-profit consulting and helping congregations. Mary was asked to do an evaluation for a women's organization and asked if she would go incognito to take notes. At one of the workshops she noticed the topic was "inner covenants".

As she sat there and Mary wasn't really paying attention to the content of the talk but concentrating on the process they had. Mary shared that she did remember the speaker saying what these inner covenants truly are. She said they are covenants, promises or decisions someone makes to themselves without including God. In other words, what you really end up doing is telling God "I will not allow anyone in that area of my heart".

So as Mary is taking notes the speaker goes on to say that she would like to pray so that God may reveal to everyone in attendance the inner covenants they may have so that He may heal them.

Everyone there bowed their heads and she saw the speaker approach her and she asked, "Do you have any inner covenants you would like to pray for?" Mary responded by saying, "Oh no…I accepted the Lord and I am filled with the Holy Spirit." The speaker responded, "Well can we just pray and ask God to reveal any possible inner covenants?" Mary said "sure why not." So she prayed a simple prayer asking God just to reveal those covenants that she may have had. No special thing.

As she prayed a thought came to Mary's mind. The woman then asked her if anything comes to mind and Mary told her of the thought from when she was a little girl when she said that she would never marry a pastor and that's what happened. So she asked if they would pray to break that covenant. Mary agreed, not thinking anything of it. She thought that was the end of it.

A month later, Mary shares that she had to visit the organization to present her results and her husband decided to join her on the trip. So they did their work and they visited their congregation and all of a sudden, her husband leans over and says to her, "What's keeping us from starting a church in our city?" Mary was a bit speechless because of his question and she asked, "Well who will be the pastors?" He responded "we can be the pastors". Mary was shocked. Well, nine months after that they founded a church in the city. Not only is she married now to a pastor but she is also a pastor."

Inner covenants, or promises made without consulting with God can affect your life, your family and those around you. Mary went on to share that her inner covenant was affecting even her husband from fulfilling his calling. As they found out some time later, he shared how an older lady had told him when he was younger that he would one day be a pastor. Without her knowing anything at that time, she was an instrument of hindrance to her husband. If you asked her what made her make that promise she would say that it was fear of the unknown, fear of the past."

God does not care about your past as much as He does your future! He knows the plan and in His plan there is no heaviness of heart. The same way Jesus asked the man by the pool at Bethesda He asks you today; "Do you want to be made well?" Again, the word "well" in New Testament Greek is *Sozo*. This means to be rescued from danger or destruction. This is God's desire for your life. He wants to rescue you from destruction and give you a fresh start. The only time God is interested in your past is to push you towards your future!

You are who God declares you to be in spite of what you have been through and what people think or say you are. I want you to understand and know who you are in Christ. You are:

- According to II Corinthians 5:17 – You are a new creation.

- According to 1 Peter 2:9 – You are a Chosen Generation, a Royal Priesthood, a Holy Nation,

His own possession.

- According to Ephesians 2:10 – You are HIS workmanship.

- According to II Corinthians 5:21 – You are HIS righteousness.

- According to John 1:12 – You are a Child of God.

- According to 1 Corinthians 6:19 - You are home to the Holy Spirit.

- According to Philippians 3:20 – You are a citizen of Heaven.

- According to John 15:15 – You are a Friend of God.

You are more than a conqueror (Romans 8:37) and filled with HIS power (Acts 1:8).

I have learned that perspective depends on where I stand. And I stand on His Word… His promises and what He says about me. My identity is the core of who I am… a constant by which I am defined, regardless of circumstances.

Proper perspective occurs when we see as God sees. We must find our identity in the One who sees as God sees. We must find our identity in Christ.

Questions to reflect on:

To who or what is my heart attached to?

Am I Heart Healthy…Spiritually?

Memory Scriptures:

Proverbs 4:23 NLT

"Guard your heart above all else, for it determines the course of your life."

Proverbs 14:30 NLT

"A peaceful heart leads to a healthy body; jealousy is like cancer in the bones."

Proverbs 15:13 NLT

"A glad heart makes a happy face; a broken heart crushes the spirit."

Proverbs 17:22 NLT

"A cheerful heart is good medicine, but a broken spirit saps a person's strength."

NOTES:

Chapter Eleven

The Metamorphosis

> *"Those who put themselves in HIS hands*
> *will become perfect, as HE is perfect –*
> *perfect in love, wisdom, joy, beauty and*
> *immorality."*
>
> C.S. Lewis Mere Christianity

We all know the process the Butterfly has to go through in order to become the stunning insect it was created to be. The first stage is the Egg stage. A butterfly starts life as a very small, round, oval or cylindrical egg. The coolest thing about butterfly eggs, especially monarch butterfly eggs, is that if you look close enough you can actually see the tiny caterpillar growing inside of it. Butterfly eggs are usually laid on the leaves of plants.

The next stage is the Larva (Caterpillar). When the egg finally hatches, most of you would expect for a butterfly to emerge, right? Well, not exactly. In the butterfly's life cycle, there are four stages and this is only the second stage. Butterfly larvae are actually what we call caterpillars. Caterpillars do not stay in this stage for very long and mostly, in this stage all they do is eat.

When the egg hatches, the caterpillar will start his work and eat the leaf they were born onto. This is really important because the mother butterfly needs to lay her eggs on the type of leaf the caterpillar will eat – each caterpillar type likes only certain types of leaves. Since they are tiny and cannot travel to a new plant, the caterpillar needs to hatch on the kind of leaf it wants to eat.

Caterpillars need to eat and eat so they can grow quickly. When a caterpillar is born, they are extremely small. When they start eating, they instantly start growing and expanding. Their exoskeleton (skin) does not stretch or grow, so they grow by "molting" (shedding the outgrown skin) several times while it grows.

Now let me pause and say that this is so cool! The Bible tells us in Matthew 6:25-26 (NASB);

"For this reason I say to you, do not be worried about your life, as to what you will eat or what you will drink; nor for your body, as to what you will put on. Is not life more than food, and the body more than clothing? Look at the birds of the air, that they do not sow, nor reap nor gather

into barns, and yet your heavenly Father feeds them. Are you not worth much more than they?"

We worry too much about things. The caterpillar has nothing to worry about because it simply knows what its purpose and process is. God created it that way…He wired it to go through a cycle just as He designed us to go through a cycle. Now the only difference is that He gave us free will and that's where we usually go wrong.

Just like the Butterfly knows where it desires to lay its eggs so our Heavenly Father knows which family and in which location He wants us to be born in. You are no mistake. You are no accident. You are *"wonderfully and fearfully made"*. People may say otherwise but God has the LAST word. Trust me, HE knew you from before the foundation of the world.

But check this next stage out. This stage is called the Pupa or what geeks call the Chrysalis. The pupa stage is one of the coolest stages of a butterfly's life. As soon as a caterpillar is done growing and they have reached their full length and weight, they form themselves into a pupa, which is also known as a chrysalis. From the outside of the pupa, it looks as if the caterpillar may just be resting, but the inside is where all of the action is. Inside of the pupa, the caterpillar is rapidly changing.

I love this. Paul is trying to teach about this kind of metamorphosing in Romans 12 when he says;

"Don't become so well-adjusted to your culture that you fit into it without even thinking. Instead, fix your attention on God. You'll be changed from the inside out. Readily recognize what he wants from you, and quickly respond to it. Unlike the culture around you, always dragging you down to its level of immaturity, God brings the best out of you, develops well-formed maturity in you."msg.

I love that! It's almost like the story I shared from John. The man by the pool was surrounded by people in the same condition as he was, lame...sick...but that is not what he was created for. We need to fix our eyes on Jesus...He makes all things new! He could have easily told Jesus, thanks but no thanks...there is no hope for me. I have been rejected too many times, hurt by almost every I came across and let in my life. I have been dumped repeatedly and talked about. Thanks for the offer Jesus but I will not let anyone else do that to me again.

Sounds familiar? Been there done that? How is this thought any different from what you are thinking? We all have gone through ups and downs in life but as King Solomon shares in the book of Ecclesiastes chapter 3, *"For everything there is a season".*

In other words, the season you are in does not have to repeat. It should have come to an end a long time ago but you continue to hold on to it. Solomon continues; *"A time to plant and a time to harvest."* You have to stop planting unhealthy seeds. Seeds of hatred because you will harvest more hurt. Seeds of bitterness, because you will harvest heart problems. Seeds of malice because you will harvest negativity. Overcome all of that today and begin to plant seeds of forgiveness…seeds of love…seeds of grace and you will harvest that which you plant.

"A time to kill and a time to heal." It is time to kill your past. It is time to kill that which has continued to hurt you. Perhaps the people you have hurt you physically or emotionally or in any other way are no longer alive and you still hold on to the things which cause you pain. You are only holding on to a memory. Let that go. Kill it today and be healed. DO NOT STAY IN THAT SEASON ANYLONGER!

"A time to tear down and a time to build up." Yes it's time to tear down the old. Out with the old in with the new. It's time to build your self-confidence. Courage and strength. *The joy of the Lord is your strength." "A time to cry and a time to laugh, a time to grieve and a time to dance."* Your pain, your sorrow, your hurt, your tears have an expiration date. But the joy of the Lord is eternal. You can laugh again…you can dance again. Let the Lord be your new dance partner.

In this stage of the Butterflies life cycle, the caterpillars are short, stubby and have no wings at all. Within the chrysalis the old body parts of the caterpillar are undergoing this remarkable transformation, called 'metamorphosis,' to become the beautiful parts that make up the butterfly that will emerge. Tissue, limbs and organs of a caterpillar have all been changed by the time the pupa is finished, and is now ready for the final stage of a butterfly's life cycle.

Psalms 139:13,15,16 (NLT) describes this process like this:

> *"You made all the delicate, inner parts of my body and knit me together in my mother's womb. You watched me as I was being formed in utter seclusion, as I was woven together in the dark of the womb. You saw me before I was born."*

Now that is pretty cool. We were created, knit together by God almighty Himself to be what He desired us to be. The process may be hard but worth it. It may sting a bit and break us in areas that need brokenness but it is not to destroy you. Allow the process for when you are done you too will realize it was worth it.

Finally, when the caterpillar has done all of its forming and changing inside the pupa, you can see the butterfly emerge. When the butterfly first emerges from the chrysalis, both of the wings are going to be soft and folded against its body. This is because the butterfly had to fit all its new parts inside of the pupa.

As soon as the butterfly has rested after coming out of

the chrysalis, it will pump blood into the wings in order to get them working and flapping – then they get to fly.

You were not created to crawl your entire life. But that is what happens when you hold on to all that weight. You cannot stand tall. You cannot fly. You are carrying too much baggage that God wants you to be free from. Lay it all down today and do that which you were created to do. You can choose to continue to crawl or you can choose to breakthrough, just like the butterfly and spread your wings and take flight! What will you do?

Questions to reflect on:

What type of seeds do I continue to plant that create an unhealthy harvest?

Why is it difficult for me to accept change?

What unhealthy habits do I need to put away from my life?

Reflection Scripture:

Genesis 12:1-3 (NIV)

> *Now the LORD said to Abram, "Go from your country and your kindred and your father's house to the land that I will show you. And I will make of you a great nation, and I will bless you and make your name great, so that you will be a blessing. I will bless those who bless you, and him who dishonors you I will curse, and in you all the families of the earth shall be blessed."*

NOTES:

Chapter Twelve

The Time Is Now

*"There's an opportune time to do things,
a right time for everything on the earth"*
Eccl.3:1 MSG

When we had arrived to Pennsylvania, we had no idea which church we would make our home church. We made several visits to a few churches but did not sense my spirit connected. As the days, weeks and months went by, we finally found our home church.

I never thought that I, a Puerto Rican from the Bronx, raised in a Pentecostal home, would ever join a non-denominational church. It was a culture shock for me at first. The worship style was different, something my wife and I were not used to. It was the same with the preaching style. But if there was anything that I was familiar with was the move of the Spirit of God. That was the same.

God began to speak to my life. One day, as I was

looking at a small gift box in my home, He spoke to me and told me, "Do you see that box. I want you to know that what you have learned about me so far is what you can fit in this box. I am more...I have more...there is more of Me for you to know and experience." I was blown away. Just when I thought I had God figured out He shows off!

There was a time when I asked my Senior Pastor, "why don't we allow the Spirit to move freely like in the old days?" His loving and gentle response was; "Did you notice the 58 souls that gave their hearts to Jesus last Sunday?" I was humbled, repentant and speechless! How was it that I missed the move of God! Again, I thought I had Him figured out. That day I repented of my ignorance.

Now, my wife and I had no plans of serving at this capacity in a church when we moved. But as the days went by I was asked to serve with the youth pastor and his team, so I did. After some time with the youth ministry I transitioned to the Spanish couple's ministry and served with them. As time went on, our Senior Pastor had a desire to begin Spanish services and asked another gentleman to lead the growing group.

What we didn't imagine was that from that small group it would turn out to be an actual Venue or Campus. In April of 2009, our Campus was birthed. Although we are now a growing and thriving congregation, this was not the case at one point. It seemed we had hit a wall. We simply were not growing. It seemed we were going the opposite direction… we were declining. Some of our leadership was struggling; my wife and I were becoming frustrated. That's when we began to pray.

We presented our petition before the Lord and we told the Lord we would give this ministry a year and if we see nothing happening I would resign as the Associate Pastor. This was in October of 2011. I recall sharing in short conversation my heart and expressed my prayer with our Senior Pastor. Needless to say, he was surprised and perhaps hurt by it.

As the months passed, I became even more frustrated and one morning with tears running down my face I was continuously asking God for direction. I told God and my wife that I would resign in November of 2012. Countless times God was trying to give me hints that a change, a shifting was about to occur but my heart was tired and frustrated.

As the end of July of 2012 approached, I was asked to join a meeting with several Pastors. I thought to myself this would be the open door for me to hand in my resignation, so I printed two letters and took them to the meeting. As I sat, my Pastor said; "Noel you thought this meeting was about the Church, and even though in part it is, it is more about you." Now that caught my attention quickly.

I was waiting for the right opportunity and I thought that this was going to be it. To my surprise, the Campus

Pastor at that time, a man of God with a great heart, shared that he was stepping down as Campus Pastor and he believed I was the right person to take the church to the next level. My jaw dropped and hit the dinner table so hard. I was speechless. It was out of left field.

I was advised to think about it and speak it over with my wife and especially to pray about it. That is what we did. Again, this is one of those moments where I thought I had it figured all out. So we as a family, decided to go on vacation and just unwind.

As we vacationed, I took some time with the Lord in the mornings during devotionals, and I would sit on the balcony of our resort and just pray. This one specific morning, I am reading the story in John 5 of the lame man by the pool at Bethesda. As I was meditating on this story God asked me the same thing He asked the man in the story. God spoke to me and asked; "Do you want to be made well." I responded, "God, What are you talking about." He said; "I want to make you well, (I desire to rescue you), but you have areas in your heart that I have not been invited into."

As I began to cry I asked God; "Help me understand." God continued to tell me; "Do you remember the letters you were going to hand in?" I said; "Yes. What about them." I stopped that from happening." He replied. God went on; "I stopped you because I wanted to work in you in order to work through you."

Many times we can hinder God's work in our lives when we attempt to do things our way... in Spanish we call that "Metiendo Las Patas". And most, if not every time, that we try to do things our way one of two things will always happen... we struggle even more, or we give up due frustration. We give up on life... on our relationships... on our ministry... on our career... on our education... and on our families.

I haven't read anywhere in scripture where God tells us to give up. On the contrary... the Bible tells us that we are more than conquerors. As a matter of fact check out what God told a guy named Joshua:

"1 After the death of Moses the servant of the Lord, the Lord said to Joshua son of Nun, Moses' aide: 2 "Moses my servant is dead. Now then, you and all these people, get ready to cross the Jordan River into the land I am about to give to them—to the Israelites. 3 I will give you every place where you set your foot, as I promised Moses. 4 Your territory will extend from the desert to Lebanon, and from the great river, the Euphrates—all the Hittite country—to the Mediterranean Sea in the west. 5 No one will be able to stand against you all the days of your life. As I was with Moses, so I will be with you; I will never leave you nor forsake you. 6 Be strong and courageous, because you will lead these people to inherit the land I swore to their ancestors to give them. 7 "Be strong and very courageous. Be careful to obey all the law my servant Moses gave you; do not turn from it to the right or to the left, that you may

be successful wherever you go. 8 Keep this Book of the Law always on your lips; meditate on it day and night, so that you may be careful to do everything written in it. Then you will be prosperous and successful. 9 Have I not commanded you? Be strong and courageous. Do not be afraid; do not be discouraged, for the Lord your God will be with you wherever you go." Joshua 1:1-7 NIV

See, the fact that you are unfamiliar with something that is happening in your life or a relationship or a new job or a career path, it does not mean that you should give up. You will never find out what your potential is or what purpose there may be in the unfamiliar until you open up and are willing to take the risk. Imagine if Joshua would have given up and said; "You know what God, Moses has died so I am done. I do not want to lead these people because I do not want to go through what Moses went through. I do not want to be criticized and mocked like Moses."

What God told me next caused the breakthrough that my life and my family's life needed. He told me; "I stopped you from becoming like your father. The decision to quit like your dad would have made you the very thing you promised yourself you would not become." WOW! God not only showed up in that resort He showed off BIG! See, you have to understand something, my dad had no one to instruct him, back him up, and support him or even to cover him. He became overwhelmed and frustrated and this was what was happening to me to certain extent.

Because that encounter at the resort was so powerful and profound for us we had to do something to remember it, like in Old Testament times we kind of built an altar… we decided to purchase a time share there! No…No… that's not the real reason.

When I was done with drying my tears and cleaning the snot from my face, I walked over to my wife to let her know what just occurred and I noticed that she was also meditating on God. Now, I never make decisions without consulting with my wife. Before I was able to speak a word, she just came out and said, "Honey, I think you should take the role as Campus Pastor. The people need someone, they need us." Once again I was speechless and that was all I needed to hear.

See one issue with many, as it was with me, is that they don't know how to wait. The Bible has over 50 scriptures that tell us to "Wait upon the Lord" or to "Be still". That is the most crucial and painful yet beneficial thing to do. One of my favorite scriptures on this subject is found in Isaiah 40:31 which says; *"But they who wait for the Lord shall renew their strength; they shall mount up with wings like eagles; they shall run and not be weary; they shall walk and not faint.*

When God says "wait", He says it because He is working in you and for you. He wants you ready for what He has for you. Allow God to make you whole. Allow Him to complete His work in your heart. Allow Him to remove the garbage that is clogging and weighing your heart so that you can run this race free from the past, free from the hurt and free from frustration. Delay doesn't mean denial!

The most recent account I have of God's faithfulness and goodness is when I was sitting in my kitchen going through my devotional and my then 8 year old son comes to me and tells me, "Dad, I know what I want to be when I am older". Now, almost every parent expects to hear, doctor, fireman, policeman or an astronaut...but that's not what my son had in mind.

I asked my son, "What do you want to be"? His response not only blew my mind but brought me to tears as well. He said, "I want to be a Pastor just like you. I want to help other kids here and around the world just like you do. I want God to use me to touch people's lives and share God with others".

My wife was sitting in the living room and when she heard that she began to cry. At first I was in shock but at the same time I was moved. Moved because I saw how God was reminding me that when He does a NEW THING it looks different, and feels different. You may not understand at first and you might have some fear but He knows where He is taking you. Just trust!

Questions to reflect on:

What do I think is holding me back from my break through moment?

Am I able to completely trust God with the inner details of my life?

Have I given up?

NOTES:

Chapter Thirteen

Take The Leap

*"It was by faith that Abraham obeyed when God called him to leave home and **go** to another land...he went without knowing where he was going."*
Hebrews 11:18 NLT

M any great men and women in the Bible or in our history have had to make a move...take a leap of faith in order to achieve the very thing that they truly believed in. We should also take that leap for our freedom...for our peace of mind and healing. We are robbing ourselves from the blessings God has for us when we don't. It may not look like the usual thing. It will look different...but that's ok. Because again, your ways are not God's ways.

God did this with Saul and David. In 1 Samuel 16 God was letting Samuel the Prophet know that He has rejected Saul (the old) as King and He has selected David (the new) as His King for the people of Israel. And when we read

1 Samuel 16:6-13 we find that God was not interested in what society deemed to be the right fit or what looked to be the favorite. He was telling Samuel that what He was choosing was going to look different.

1 Samuel 16:6-13 (NASB) *"6 When they entered, he looked at Eliab and thought, "Surely the Lord's anointed is before Him." 7 But the Lord said to Samuel, "Do not look at his appearance or at the height of his stature, because I have rejected him; for God sees not as man sees, for man looks at the outward appearance, but the Lord looks at the heart." 8 Then Jesse called Abinadab and made him pass before Samuel. And he said, "The Lord has not chosen this one either." 9 Next Jesse made Shammah pass by. And he said, "The Lord has not chosen this one either." 10 Thus Jesse made seven of his sons pass before Samuel. But Samuel said to Jesse, "The Lord has not chosen these." 11 And Samuel said to Jesse, "Are these all the children?" And he said, "There remains yet the youngest, and behold, he is tending the sheep." Then Samuel said to Jesse, "Send and bring him; for we will not sit down until he comes here." 12 So he sent and brought him in. Now he was ruddy, with beautiful eyes and a handsome appearance. And the Lord said, "Arise, anoint him; for this is he." 13 Then Samuel took the horn of oil and anointed him in the midst of his brothers; and the Spirit of the Lord came mightily upon David from that day forward."*

In verse 13, God tells Samuel to anoint David who is to be the next King. I learned that from the time that

David was anointed until the time He was appointed there was a fifteen year gap. During that time there was a process that he had to go through. Perhaps you are in the beginning, in the middle or towards the end of a process. You have heard a promise or several promises from God but have not seen them fulfilled yet. Don't sweat it. God has your back.

If He calls you He will provide for you. He doesn't call without a plan! I dare say that He knows what He is doing simply because He has been doing it since…umm well… eternity! You can be assured that if He said it He will do it; If He spoke it He will bring it to pass! You can trust His Word more than the word of your local weather reporter!

I never thought I would hear my son tell me that He wants to be a Pastor when he is older. It shows God's faithfulness to His Word. Just when I thought he was going to say something I expected, God does something totally different! Not only is He providing for me but He is dealing with me and allowing me to leave a legacy for my children and my children's children. And I have much work to do in order for that legacy to continue. I must instruct my children and show them to love God and serve people. How do I do this? By living it out and showing my kids how to live for God not simply by telling them but by showing them.

I searched online to see how the human heart was formed. I was reading on all of its ins and outs. A particular area in the heart which is called the "Atrium" caught my attention. This particular area deals with the blood. Here is a quick description of what it is.

"In anatomy, the atrium (plural: atria) is a portion of the blood collection chamber of the heart. The atrium is a chamber in which blood enters the heart, as opposed to the ventricle, where it is pushed out of the organ. It has a thin-walled structure that allows blood to return to the heart. The atrium receives blood as it returns to the heart to complete a circulating cycle, whereas the ventricle pumps blood out of the heart to start a new cycle." (Atrium (heart) from Wikipedia, the free encyclopedia).

Here are several definitions given by dictionary.com for "atrium":

1. **Architecture:**

   a. Also called Cavaedium. The main or central room of an ancient Roman house, open to the sky at the center and usually having a pool for the collection of rain water.

   b. A courtyard, flanked or surrounded by porticoes, in front of an early or medieval Christian church. See diag. under basilica.

   c. A sky lit central court in a contemporary building or house.

2. **Anatomy:** either of the two upper chambers on each side of the heart that receive blood from the veins and in turn force it into the ventricles.

Now this is very interesting because the Tabernacle described in Exodus 36 – 40, also had an Atrium. And in this Atrium was a basin which was used to cleanse those that would serve in the Tabernacle such as Aaron and his sons. It happened that once a year the High Priest would enter the Holy of Holies to make sacrifice on behalf of the people and in order to enter he first had to be cleansed. This cleansing occurred in the Atrium.

The Atrium represents Christ. He stands between us and God the Father and He says in His Word, "I am the way, the truth and the life and no one can come to the Father except through me" (John 14:6). This is so cool because no matter what we are struggling with or have held on to for so long we NOW know how to be cleansed and freed from it. We know now that we can come to the Father through Jesus Christ Himself.

Check out my friend Lisa's story (not her real name). Lisa a dear friend of ours and our Spiritual daughter who came to our church broken, hurt, and insecure. Read how God transformed her heart. How she let go of her past.

Lisa, a young thirty two year old, had lived a good part of her life with hurt and pain but God has been her strength and shield. Today this young lady is both happy and joyful. But is wasn't always like this.

She was born into a Christian home. Her parents taught her the fear of the Lord. As this young girl grew up she began to have issues at the church she grew up in. When she began to attend High school she thought she found the love of her life. A young Christian boy who was pretty smart and caring.

Now, this is pretty much how a lot of young teenage girls see things. A cute and intelligent boy shows up, he dazzles her and boom. Girls...KEEP YOUR GUARD UP AND NEVER COMPROMISE IN THIS AREA OF YOUR LIFE!

This young couple now began to live a life of sin and became sexually involved and all of a sudden, what happens with almost every young couple that lives in sin and gets sexually involved, happened with this couple... she became pregnant. This was a huge blow to this young girl, for she was only seventeen years old. Neither of them, just as any teenager, were prepared for this so they both decided not to have the baby. They planned this together needless to say, the child didn't live.

As months went by so much guilt was on their shoulders because of what they had done. And they knew it was a serious sin. They continued to live together, until the news hit... she was pregnant again. This time they both decided to keep the child and to get married. The day arrived where a beautiful little baby girl filled the lives of these two families.

Lisa's life was going well. She and her husband returned to church. Just five months after her child was born they come to find out that Lisa was expecting yet again. This time she took the news hard. She was only nineteen years old and was going to be a mother of two.

Sometime later Lisa's husband decides to join the Military to try a make a better life for his Young family... and this is where the nightmare begins.

After completing his training he returns home to his family. Lisa excitedly welcomes the love of her life home as he deserved, but she had no idea what was to transpire. This young husband was completely a different person. He began became abusive, not only physically but verbally as well. He began to have affairs with other women. Just when she thought everything was going great, it was turning out to be a nightmare for her. All was well from the door to the outside but when you walked in to the house it was a different story.

This young lady would pray to God that He would change her husband, she could not believe that the love of her life, the man whom she would write songs for, would treat her like this. This abuse went on for five years and Lisa decided that she would stay quite through it all. The moment Lisa understood that he was not going to change she decided she was going to end this relationship. But she had no idea that decision would cause greater pain, not only for her, but also for her daughters.

At this point she had nowhere to turn but to God as her refuge. Waiting on God isn't the easiest thing but with time you find out that He will give you strength.
She was determined and as she began to seek the Lord more she saw how God was by her side. As she sought the Lord, she prayed that God would heal her and set her free.

Sometime after, she met a young man who came into her life while she still had bitterness in her heart toward her ex-husband. But this young man was willing to stick by her side and even father her two daughters.

This couple decided to begin their lives somewhere new. They had no clue where they would end up. But God knew. This couple was going through struggles as well. She even considered divorcing him because she always thought he too would one day treat her the same way her last husband treated her and she could not handle that again.

Once they moved, she went online and found our church. She came to our church with her family, and from that day on, she shares that she and her family are forever grateful to God for her Pastors and her new church family who have welcomed them and adopted them as their own.

This young woman has experienced and encountered God's love like never before along with His forgiveness. She shares, "I am living with a new heart, forgetting the past and what caused me pain. I can worship God with passion and love my husband more and more each day. I can love and care for my daughters as well without heaviness of heart." ONLY GOD CAN DO THAT!

The scripture that ministered to this young woman when she heard me preach for the first time was John 11:40; *"Then Jesus said, "Did I not tell you that if you believe, you will see the glory of God?"* She says that this is the scripture she clings to.

I pray that everyone that is going through or has gone through these similar situations will make it theirs as well.

This young woman could have remained a slave to her past. See, many, perhaps even you, have built walls and created a prison for yourself. You created it using bricks. Those bricks have a specific name… hurt… hatred… bitterness… anger… unforgiveness… fear… low self-esteem… resentment… etc…

Only you know the names of those bricks which have formulated your prison. Now you feel trapped and helpless. But today I have great news… IT'S NOT OVER!

I have learned that the Chinese, when describing something they use characters. And the characters they use for the word "difficulty" is a two part word… "Danger" and "Opportunity".

Today you get to choose if you will remain in "danger" or use this as an "opportunity" to break through… take the leap… transform your life… and move forward in the name of Jesus!

As I look back at the challenges my wife and I had gone through, I could only thank God for providing the strength He provided. But we cannot keep our focus on the things of the past. Our eyes stay fixed on Jesus and Jesus is always moving forward therefore so should we.

When I read the story of Abraham (Abram at that time) in Genesis chapter 13 verses 14-17 (Para-phrase mine), God speaks to Abram after his nephew Lot had decided to go to different land, and God tells Abram; "Look as far as you can see in every direction – north, south, east and west. I am going to give you all the land you see, to you and your descendants as a permanent possession. And I will give you so many descendants that, like the dust of the earth, they cannot be counted." But here is the interesting part…after God tells Abram I am going to give it to you…He then tells Abram in verse 17… "GO and Walk through"! God wants you to know that He is offering you a BREAKTHROUGH but it is up to you to GO and WALK through!

We have been blessed and favored simply because of

our obedience to Go and Walk through. Because of His grace and because we have decided to let Him create a new heart in us, we have seen His hand work on our behalf for His Glory. You can experience the same…you can experience your breakthrough today.

Allow Him to give you a new heart today. Allow the lessons and the stories in this to book become your story of freedom and breakthrough. Only Jesus can give that to you. Nothing else in this world can provide what only God can provide. I invite you to pray this prayer as I end this story:

God my Father, I thank you in this moment for allowing me to understand that all you want to do is love me unconditionally. Thank you for the sacrifice of your Son Jesus. Forgive me for ignoring you and running from you, whether it was knowingly or unknowingly. Cleanse me and create in me a new heart. Guide my decisions as you are right now. Write my name in the Lambs book of life. I accept Jesus as my Lord and my Savior. Give me Your Heart beat. Help me to see those areas in my heart that need healing, repair and restoration. Help me to forgive those who have done me harm. I want to be free and I want to set them free. I pray for your light to shine in me and through me. I thank you and honor you right now. In Jesus name…AMEN!

If you made this prayer for the first time I would like to hear from you…

Please write me at <u>ConditionsOfTheHeart@gmail.com</u> and tell me your story.

NOTES

A Very Special Thanks

All glory, all honor and thanks to my Lord, my Savior Jesus. The sacrifice on that cross for me was the greatest gift ever! Without that gift, I would not have known what living is. Thank you for your faithfulness, the hope you provided, your grace and the Salvation of my soul and above all Your Love!

To my beautiful wife Kayla: you have stuck by my side through it all and for many years. You were my partner then and you continue to be my partner now. I am a blessed man, husband and father because of you. I am amazed to know that you were there when God placed the calling in my life over 20 years ago and how today you are a part of that journey and calling...GOD IS GOOD! Who would have guessed that God had this planned for us? I love you babe.

To my children Jared Noel and Jaden Jewels; thank you for your smiles. That I am able to come home to two amazing gifted kids and also for putting up with all the work and time that went into this project. My prayer is that you will both walk in integrity and that you will always have the Lord's guidance. I love you both.

My Senior Pastor and one of my greatest mentors, Randy Landis, Sr. You have challenged me and have given me the opportunity to grow by planting seed through Godly instruction and teaching. Throughout the years you have caused a greater desire in me to seek God and His word more and more. I can truly say that I have seen you pour your heart selflessly into young men like myself simply to see them flourish into what God has called them to be.

My father Rosendo and my mother Marta…it all started with your love. Thank you for your long hours of prayer and support. You never gave up on us and for that I am forever grateful.

To my friend and Spiritual father and mentor, Rev. David Serrano, Sr. I love you, I appreciate you and honor you for the sixteen plus years you challenged me and allowed me to labor under your ministry. I have learned so much from you. Forever grateful for you and your family.

Thank you to my Lifechurch family for your support, for your prayers, for believing, inviting, and allowing us to serve. Many hearts have been transformed and many more to go.

Mike Rivera thank you for believing in me and in this

project. You were the first to encourage me and to assist me in all the details and I am forever grateful.

And last but not least...Thank you to all our family and friends, you are all greatly appreciated.

Notes

1   De La Mora, Sergio, 1966, The heart Revolution (Gran Rapids, MI; Baker Publishing Group)

2   ZONDERVAN, What on earth am I here for? Pg.23; The Purpose Driven Life, Copyright © 2002, 2011, 2012 by Rick Warren)